The Islands

WITHDRAWN

John Sakkis

The Islands

Nightboat Books
New York

ISBN: 978-1-937658-26-7

Cover: Pablo Guardiola, *I wish to communicate with you, K/Kilo*, 2011.
C-print, 28 x 42 inches. Courtesy of the artist.

Design and typesetting by Margaret Tedesco
Text set in Plantin and Helvetica Neue

Cataloging-in-publication data is available
from the Library of Congress

Distributed by University Press of New England
One Court Street
Lebanon, NH 03766
www.upne.com

Nightboat Books
New York
www.nightboat.org

For my Mom, Carol Ann Sakkis

1/
A Large Population Of Antiques

one night, after the happily of dinner, after they hadn't been found for sometime later, but only the one's who found this, one of them was thinking about the toy car brought to his skin, which was given, "to feel the cold wheels spin" they said "on your forearm, on your back" they said "come to the table" "meet your cousins"

you can't skip a rock through
the house without starting fires

you can't set fire to the beach
in the afternoon without boats

the house was a slobbering white giant
moving its bowels throughout the summer

the beach is an even playing field for
insects, cousins and boats

there are deserted beaches in the movies
meaning the fields are dirty but remain burning

the entire hotel is only accessible by
boat or on foot, a small bay brings
law and order to the beaches

you can't skip a rock through
this wealth of water without surrendering
the afternoon, every meal ends up
destroying boats with fires

the two boys like a scrim of giant wings backing away from that serrated phrase "happily" in the field the boys play with barbed wire on top of the table small fish fried with bread and oil out of the movies setting the long table with their own juices and bones to choke down before the boys find their seats taking as long as they can hunting insects in olive trees the orchard feels cool and wooden stuffing the white-roe under the house the mud is a toy perfect for starting wars with this scrim furiously pulled out in strands from their backs this gossamer wall setting the table into a fortress on four legs

The Cousins Sang an Insect Pastoral

The cousins sang an acre, a warehouse
A rock skipped across its belly bursting
A thick red fire, we collect snails
In the orchard eating, marble
In the summer as slick as snow melting
The summerhouse naps and snails
Still stewing, eating, verdant insects chirping
So much that, like the fishmonger
They double as smell

A Diasporic Royal Complex

closer than nimbus
fortnight column and
the whispering couldn't better
a bellow night or
because of this church chant
"I profile the usual explanation for"
this water being the warehouse
which carried the goods
for patterns sake
whole families
sitting around a room
which carried his voice
to his parent probably
asking, in addition "when
do we eat lunch?"
by night being eaten as well
for whatever it's worth
next to the bed
I wouldn't sleep anyway
for the foreign sailors
it cannot be proved
these clothes were being
tucked among discos
a slow disintegrate siesta
the strobe lights
that ground any winged insect
upon touching

regarding solutions
and months of days
behind his priest drinking beer
that catapult dangerously closer
to ear drum stuck with mucus
as if his ears were telling him
that no human should be willing
to travel at such ridiculous heights

and only here with a red bike at least the night of such a dock were the nails
holding up such tan legs and onetime the scrotum of a local boy was seen
dangling near his thigh as he ran the hair curling up in damp clumps as salt
floating without the thousands of jellyfish washed up but still potent as an
iron would sting if brushed against the hair of his arm

such moths without sleeping
and days of one eminent
by means of/ with scenes
of the box too mistaken
by hearing the chants at night
rather to get the pieces at
the right time among others
at a glance of what other
people could see they were ivory
steps an ivory desk only color
an ivory slip his shared interests
ivory time around the turn
a small book of tangrams
and correspondents facile
traces against rolling feet
square the body top spinning
full leads solved in seconds
the most boyish maneuver
or fewer strokes is called a "portes"
break in the ear and the warm
delicate hands of a cloth

one header said
note the book "flash in the pan"
becoming the pores of the tongue
were large and gray thrust to
inspecting in the mirror in the cheeks
also was a silver crack of pores
edging only that bifurcated
sliver and he said "watch the marble as it goes"
slipping onto its steps that conference building
meeting the mayor who began to say
his favorite city the White City
and the water bringing a warehouse
of clouds about the television crew
and his interviewing "as the white city"
almost always relying on the organ of others
as it goes with those boys at the hotel
and marble steps rolling into the peeling
tits of swimming laps and "from the Bay"
not bulging Chapel Hill who said it
was a photo of girls doing aerobics
at the Hotel Alevas kicking
ancient rubber from under their feet

Athens this time

that lower lounge

the pagan faced bathhouse

playing soccer

one proceeds by the

daughters in ground

hatched sperm and

the White Tower

bury the baked salmon

"the priceless hole [sic] of century"

knot exactly

Alexander The Great

boasts back to the cradle of civilization
I forget not only eye-shadow
but a broad streaked shoulder plate
how vaporous and trippy
flat "like a 'Dutch-face'" she said
drooling over the marble-lined
reception room
a tongue-garden of grilled installations
but only partly cooked

that the spider wasn't a spider at all but a tick foraged from the ground that
soon would be swallowing our cousin who slapped it off an arm only after
tearing up the courtyard tearing out his liver

Pacific In A Dare, In Love

there is still prejudice when
the trend-following flying fish of Phylakopi
hide behind ancient stone fortifications
begging to become blue ankle tattoos

made public
the safety
of seams
they drove
went mad
the ride
of bass

STAINS

1.   in actuality these accidents are not at all uncommon
at Lime Ridge
we found a fig bush
and picked it
and filled bags with it
and most of it
was rough

"history of seedling and seduction"

the sea they swam in from dock to dock
a spatial attention and the white dust of salt
coating their bellies until lunch and the summer
home trail that dreaming insect became "bare
ruined choirs" upon first noticing the difference
in size of bottle one could never imagine "other
bottles of testament" humming into the draft

for centuries these
bodies
slam around
a large population of antiques
great dunce
cap of all time
lurking
figures there
who speak a savory minimalism
as they swim their
cotton underwear bubbles to the surface

—I've never seen legs as girlish as these

—I come from Laconia, I want you out of my house

when I go traveling in

the horse-saddle shaped universe

it was clear to me "this state of emergency"

for example, one is forced

to include this lyric from

that pop song, it is surprising

that this lyric should be more complicated

the more public it is, and simpler

the more private it is

—but this minimalism fixes the emergency itself

into another house

IT DOES NOT DO THAT

Online Traffic School

that he apologized after shining the mag light into my eyes was-written-on-
photo
$2 out the door we cut out written-on-photo

fishy mornings
our uncle
Richea
a Passover
at the computer lab
this sea-brine
"because my computer tends to kick me off-line"

online this was being stated: Your thumbprint or fingerprint, if you have no
thumbs, will be taken.

and further: Throughout this course, the term "thumbprint" will be used to
mean a thumbprint or finger print, if you have no thumbs.

you've already booked the hostels that you will be staying in

2/
Leon Sakkis

and what can a New Collective encounter but the reorganization in which
identity becomes a group in a drop-in-on-a-cold-afternoon sort of way

basically benign people in a well-coordinated, yet often lonely
social world

and if "I even voted,"
maintain that at least

Archimedes had it, a charm-mechanism
that wasn't proved until

Legend has it that in 212 B.C. when the Romans besieged the Greek city of Syracuse, Archimedes set fire to the invading fleet with an array of mirrors. In 1973, at a naval base near Athens, a Greek engineer named Ioannes Sakkis attempted to determine whether this was possible using 50 to 60 bronze mirrors pointed at a rowboat more than 50 metres out in the Bay. In less than two minutes, the target was ablaze.

JUNE 14th 1944
JUNE 14TH 1944
june !$TH !($$

he could membrane that song enflamed
red fog on a corner
overlooking the weather
he couldn't find the backgammon board
and made his mind up to set the
game in an ally
the red fog, hands wringing
for a definition,
Portes means "door"

SYRACUSE
ΠΟΡΤΕΣ

on the face

of a friend

the eggs

on the rug

in the room

who would've thought he woulda been seen (this popular) in this story

with mud on his face

2. Upon a Bone But Narrowly Led

salt and fish
a bony wish
in the "dial-up are you kidding"
upon a bone
of the training
of memory-based learning
is performed and Georgios Sakkis
lists with intense traffic
ing in mothballs for further
trafficking of terror
the anti-spam will be better
the mayor or anti-spam
inspection would be
an eatery but also
Greeks signing out

who introduced MAC-better *Ling-Spam*
"a publicly cost-sensitive collection of Mac-
better and legitimate from a mailing list on Mac-
better" upon a salt of water
a slick

compared with Naive Bayes filter
who remarked that this wasn't such
a common name to in previous
"where are you from's?" and is viable
upon a bone
that you would be writing me this letter
never heard of your similar behavior
version of the k-Nearest Neighbor says
meet me on Paraskevi to discuss your name
(janky in many places) further
we swam the live long day
upon a salt-lick
of better-machines

FUNNIES

OMG! says **"SYRACUSE"** i've never had a first MAC-better, hence, a *memory-based* anti-spam if we could only go to Delos and be in many cases Delos they can be computationally "I wish you wouldn't speak that way in front of (C.W.) and (S.D.)" though for sitting there rather than, in much more detail, saying it.

BOTH BOTH says **"SYRACUSE"** in Benchmark corpus though we shouldn't compete, less topic-specific than one might expect, such as the Reuters corpora we could find my family in the *MANGAS* Port though of course *Ling-Spam* was never actually called this. What is Slump, what is Sucka Free, what is C-town, what is HYPHY (at HTML), what is Studio-Gangsta?

he was commonly looking for an answer to his question
that this could possibly be a common problem/ happily
that I could possibly have an answer for him if
he just looked, or typed in the right address

as he was wearing his sweaty armpits as he read this
\\\\

salt or,

apostle of salt

The DJ Archimedes Screw

one of his BLOCKBUSTAH
a large array of mirrors
(you touch him, and he mimes)
lifts water to higher levels
for irrigation often and
pavola with berries and
whipped cream
so you're probably off with
a "hang-loose" hand
drinking to introduce
the first white-
headed inferno
located next to invading Romans
furiously whipping a carafe of retsina
that he could take a marble-topped table
and be on the same television as that
surgeon with a sprinkling
of oregano and rolling sands
to fork out this ancient surgeon who
performed (SCULLY)/ I know what you're thinking
I burst into tears
I feared surgery
as a castaway
she kissed forgeries
on his force
"so his death may have been
BOUT retribution"

SYRACUSE

Leon Sakkis was among several Jewish resistance fighters in action against German military units. On the night of June 14, 1944 he was killed by machine gun fire as he was trying to help a wounded colleague.

10superscript64

FUNNIES

OMG! says **"SYRACUSE"** so sincerity from the Roman General-sack/ I guess I just trust that boxing is more than provocation from the Roman General-axis/ and/ and told this story/ naturally I'm just kissing (A.W.)/ during a battle.

BOTH BOTH says **"SEAPORT"** understand this is BURNER replying/ a single rope pulling to have discovered the GATE at which his Theo would be picking them up where has Dino gone, where is the phone booth, you're not my aunt whereby the hosts would be fixing us GAME RELATED also known as "you're doing a good thing, you're making us all proud, now eat your tomatoes."

HE IS REPUTED TO HAVE HELD THE ROMANS
TO A PILLAR ON DELOS

Burning days of the year under burning ferry
The biggest and brightest sink-hole churning
Crab-apple orchard among other trees banishing
Prickly stems mashed in the cracks with boats
Or moths, an abandoned airport, the salty conditions
Of the darkest voyages, the south-western
red-lights, bark-trees, or smoke reeling
About the mast with small windows
Opened, or occurring as treasure is
Guarded with labyrinthine consistency

WHEREBY THE
////
FOLKERS
"by using a large array of "it's all good"

NATHAN ONE OF HIS OFF THE CHAIN

to post notices

a show of these

music acts

she said "enjoy your time"

and world music acts

carved into the scenic

performances of Herodes Atticus

over views of the city at sunset

reader VI/ it's

top quality Greekness and well worth it

the main Olympic stadium

also runs performances

hosting shows from the likes of

a haunting, beautiful

southern wind

in the dark

coastal clubs and cafés

the competitors here

are the biggest and best

a hotbed, a leather-clad force

in mid-July, and at its sunniest

seems like a Hollywood premier

a made-for-HBO-

bordeaux where serious

music lovers get geeky

over the soundsystem

but regarding the moths by the colored strobe lights a beach could swim a cylinder on the way to making milky parts, the cylinder that couldn't dance as well as find out about the garbage strike, the white bar where they would be hard as ACORN ARCHIMEDES and a balloon-and-fairy-light-filled-courtyard

They Sang A Soccer Song

so as to provide shelter
space bodied forth
not yet hovering
not yet shining
a bumbling force
the rock
on

Off The Hinges

I came up shaking
Spying stocks of stocks
They teem
A little wood room
Made narrowest

Or the flock of a wheel
They return and spin
Before midnight

In the benthos
Barefoot
The boiling water
Spinning like a pillar

He would mistake this for honey

And sear his tongue

Across the tip

Blue-fish hanging

Above his ankles

The grip
Of Athens
"like a dog" she said
Fish meat of sleep

3/
Tangrams The New Collective

"Farewell, cousin, here we're frozen."

after Bhanu Kapil
RIP Jimmy Lopez

The House of Matters

Frigate came here, nodding for worm. A soil I may shove into my tract: (The Funnies) how free Benjamin is, if he hadn't picked the STOMA, having noticed PINK to UVP rays, aging special effect around the edges, able to, you'll see, you can make a comeback.

                    (speaking of the "don't worry, babe,": very bare-a blue tongue, from old-fashioned bathroom salts.
A barely yellow dimly-lit back room, from suckling a married woman's—
6 ounces for legs that smear beaches, in an English (Mother's story) white paper bag
no bigger than the O, the "big-O" that's an hard "O"—))
        Oh tried, I went in, PG to see if the worm was in the jar. Collecting myself, a
boy, after downing a drink
                    "YOU'RE INNOCENT WHEN YOU DREAM."

(he said) (the bar is packed)

Red lighting, colored-tiles and a wall paper sized picture of the city the
Greeks still call Constantinople

(a real girl) in this old candle-lit house

       otherwise its got smoke stained walls, the worm on tiny café tables,
it was a dream I'd been in

earlier: Off The Richter: (and the moon hits) lit by flickering candles, and a
chewed-up tart

of prose, these nude photos, long hair, this convenient classic movie "*Her
hair is straight, the hair is straight and remarkably sharp.*" This place is an island
but delightfully social. Flaky hunks of baklava return home as ancient fish
scales of steel-and-stone.

This was the city's edge. "Farewell, cousin, here we're frozen."

Even the café-worm can justly claim credit

authentic antiques happily beginning to transform, showcasing storefronts.

       (his sandals are still the best you'll find in Athens)

The salt of human projects. I

could see trash art to photographs of Iraqi children to a European Jazz
Festival

happily led/ red-fog

this permanent exhibit   .

whorls. Once, I was between living

art and nightlife

found with skin: it kick-started in leather sandals

a little parody, in such a project your haggling skills,

and a bottle of Ouzo will get you something you never knew you needed.

When I played Byzantine chants

the worm would daub her privates at every moment, by deportation of this
frigate salt, that stung.

he sang
"To the ceiling
Which prefers
War and exile
He is still barred
Yet still barred
Yet in a world
And the city
"Swept all its singers away
And the city
"Between a million birds and pictures
we made toasts
in my mouth
in my blood"

SYRCACUSE

MERKury, ASPHALT, the sudden suction where friends could hear his funeral and hear California, hear C-Town because nobody resembles nobody.

His departure of faith, he was the cousin of S.L. and L.L.. Laughing for one brief passage then he ended up in the Co Co Times obituary, he ended up there a very ordinary species, we drank Amador's moonshine at Amador's wedding, a few passages later found him saying "you left, you left, don't worry we got it," a woman and a man is an emphasis making a "stage" to weep and play not hesitating to display C-Town spirit in clairvoyance or only his thought very well, his tender-organs: embalmed and bleeding.

Gone. He is here now. A bit rowdy. When I go in heat. When I am offended by strangers.

It seems like a natural end. Someone girly in their own right, someone happily.

I go in. I am in bits.

And then it traces its own. Falls somewhere close to "any thought can be kin to another."

What happened in the House Of Matters, "Farewell, cousin, here we're frozen."

I'm able to be sure

in this role of oxygen.

4/
The Islands

Naxos

move if you can makeout her mouth sort of miming to B.B. happy birthday
and handing him a bottle which is to illustrate the progress of civilization up
to the present day that I was there when bought in Greek four packets of
Karelia's Virginia and brought back a big bottle fit for treason, stratagem, and
spoils knocking the ball against the little house where I was born beginning
to see that "two ugly make a pretty" moving upwards of a crooked village
road not ten miles from the mud baths we read about as well as a foundry,
coal-breaker, machine-shops, and light-house

STOMACHION

the strips of paper could be assembled in the shape
of a Penobscot
this retro detail
at the Omonia station
makes for a leisurely BAY in battle

"it is a place
dissolving our relatives
in the warm
funeral that roots them
the scavengers came
so quickly
and he was embarrassed
and wrote it down
perhaps too quickly"

"the fixer" in there would be plenty
of moths around his dignity

whistling, charging, calling, eraser, musical, horns, rampage, country, chief, believed, of both, prince, wielder, so extensive, fortune, pervin', tools, 1615, scalped, this word comes from the, fortune, barney, saw chase, breezy, fortune, they could, chopper, GREAT SPIRIT, for reals?, in their dealings, now Augusta, now Piraeus, NOW ATHENS, NOW CONCORD, NOW GEOGRAPH, EPA city, FA SHOO, Maine Indians, have not given, NOTICE, Janky////

the fixer
sits on the shoulder
GIANTS
taking notice
the way names' seem
to change in this town
every now and then
they have a name
for the park that
they play in
to sculpt
the way we look

FROM THE HEIGHT OF THE HIGHWAY

when we drive on beaches
it's hard to s(and) the sight,
that rotating stable

of landscapes we enter
define our
erotic needs

Delos

after I woke up and thought how strange it was not to feel ashamed of this feeling that maybe I could actually kiss her and not be so worried about dreaming or dreams as strangers with something wielding from their content even if perhaps only momentarily strangers or the marks of roses a diffusion that soaks up detail like remember the band the boy plays in as a hill with rocks bifurcated on foggy strangers and shadows collected in grammar exuberantly articulate and wet in the mouth forming portraits of strangers

Athens began "I'm sorry you had to see it like this" "it lies with us for this masquerade to change meaning" and further "first, we must use words that magnify," to get an Athens effect on the job, his foreskin in her hand though surely Athens furthers "you mean into reality? what of it? let them try," we're sitting here with my cousin, her freckled shoulder framed by freckled lips

"a mouth's a moth that can burn no further"

THIS IS MUNI, WE ALL HAVE OUR HORRORS

rapture this audition, ululate does it feel to live in petrified Concord, on the pillar written "we do find images of nude women," Athens began again, "what will she do," and further, "she'll sing from a pillar, that's all," though surely Athens furthers, "I love you because you're tender and sweet, you the hardest and sternest of men," it's this audition ululate, that's perhaps of a dog and his doggerel biology, a memory made of predicable dog like qualities

there are no bruises
the people were all inanimate
and darkness is filling the shoe

Evia

saddle-burr covering
her legs, fried sea-weed
going to port
O dancing local fish
taking in the free show
terrific sleep singing
rebetiko to the tune
of this leafy Northern
neighborhood

OMG! says "**Athens**" the last thing I expected when I started this thing was to get remarks like, "Farewell, cousin, here we're frozen," and why would I want to keep doing that thing that takes, by the way, about 2 1/2 hours every time I sit down to do it? Without them I'd be nothing and you hold that against me.

BOTH BOTH says "**Athens**" Athens says I had the presence

of mind to make
her one of our saints.

But then the whole
business is starting
all over again.   "Farewell, cousin"
To Portland to Bigga Bay by being transmetropolitan walking around with a curled lip and sock em' fists when Athens says "You belong to the court

describe to me
exactly

in the center those
who are still with me
are ready to die for me   by ORIGIN."

Asclepius

around his snake or boxes and bundles of pleading or blisters at the foot
of the hill he built a track and the scent of mulled dressings at the sharp
skull of his arch that binds, unpacks an injury of sweat to the floor of Gods
and Globes

/he who has reaped the river/
tiny globes scatter

after LRSN

she came to the door with a
stick and hit it with a
gentle-rap that made an
indian-song and the debris
that flew from her stick hit a
dog in the ear with a range
of motion not seen since a
dog-star day

Olynthus

and if you see "VS." on a flier know this means spinning TOGETHER

wait, cracking sea-salt anemone in fist, in palm
in "what you should taste is because she likes to collect hundreds at one visit"
going for hundreds of EURO at a time
in my fist I spoon a stick-full of orange jelly
from her palm and mouth it as tasting mango
in the mouth more sweet than B.B. said "I should have tried it."

The Mirror Is Hell

—Sundowner Graffiti

goes the bones
on the brick
of the throat
in the fig
goes the lethe
of ouzo

—dedicated to the person that I particularly want
to look into it—

Santorini

"Hyphen's Hyphen" Hyphy
after Susan Gevirtz

greenflies curling
the watch pulls
swimming
our Blue-fish
caught
or broke
"these busy insects"
my hair knotted
and salty
the way we sun ourselves

AUF DER HACKERBRUKE (120 m)

Mykonos

we explored them with great relish an obvious fascination for these generous
bottles of retsina to post up our hut with two wicker chairs and tackling
this yet unsolved problem of moving some girls who were "crazy as a bat"
sketched with sufficient boldness to find a construction of horses and riders
clearly as legible as the dogs and foxes barking their way through those white
alleys and little groupings to give it scope

he could hear the same ballad
on all the radios

from the same ballroom
with yellows and oranges

Athens

for Siarita Kouka

the Eve image
the playing board
rectangle of fabric
return of the dead
go-get-'em spirit
no longer the referent
and the person
salty as the rook
moving pieces
along the photo
the totemic and marble
gesture always
apricots and sea-salt
or Olynthus
and Aegean
went wrestling
with his namesake

Piraeus

"Mad—bad—and dangerous to know" bore George Gordon to the pageant of his bleeding heart in Philhellenic pirated by radicals reaching further and further to Cephalonia devoted to his fortune and the shaft that paid the brigade a remedy of bleeding heroism on hearing the news the Carbonari dreaming *The Two Foscari* to beat the row and lasting eulogy "she walks in beauty" at the crack of bark the bloody news spoke for many writing on a rock "Byron is dead" and agreed to act as the agent on VIRONOS he became a name not an island and subjugated to "Byron is dead" "so, we'll go no more a-roving" immense and lasting.

5/
The Moveable Ones

eight years
before the coin-baller
comes and returns
those fixins
that uncrowned
gold coin/ bothersome bluebird
because of you
I'm full of care
and wanting to
smith the stake
while downplaying
"the great indignity
of being kept
in the hospital for
an ingrown toenail"

I weighed 95 pounds
and stunk
the "Resident 'goes' Rational"
prior to uploading

"Write this. We have burned all their villages."

in C-Town the antiques
are fixin'
and the Transbay Tube
is as wet in its depth
as its died
a Roman Catholic
offering of
bulls, abyss
is abbey, harnessing
wet with
water the least
detail you already
know "move their
feet under their seats"
and behind them
that D-boy coils his whip
ing his best dog
of souls

"the islands will
be a grave
for their children"

which slept inside
the rock
which the mind
is made up
which exenterates
the islands
and then and then
so it became
an immediate rime

which they will forget
in a sense
then go to sleep

…

"the limit of the song is this
prelude to a journey to
the outer islands"

his words are over
the stain on the sheet

the flower and so on
the ink dries

to the piles
of flowers

and antiques

which are also opal
a long blue

listeners at the crook
of the brook

...

I have been traveling
a white strip
my head is the meadow
the carnelian
weather or
a small room in
a steel vise
I am a woman or
a boat traveling
into the details
as it sounds
to fuck the
subject against
the ceiling
of the bathroom
sulfur borders
mirroring the brides
waved an "odor of sulfur
penetrated the room"

The Moveable Ones
after Michael Palmer

Soaps, of sweat, the baker
amongst shades, and folly.
Yesterday you met a young Benjamin
over soapy Turkish coffee.

All talk of skulls.

Soaps, of sweat, and Baker
in San Francisco the bridges'
semi-satiric vein. Blogging.
The most striking, bare skulls
as well. The day-glow
of bridges
in the shape of Star Wars
that of head to ass makes
excellent a standard

both enjoined the fear
that of scalp to ass fluctuates
and was later merged
We are at war
near our face

of the Bay, the soaps,
of sweat, cracks the skull
in Athens the agora
of Lucian's
Dialogues of the Dead
you seem to think
ing provides servile
as well. We are at war
on the floor how vivid
at times, and the marble
not the dignity
that's called a date

quite often take fright
and my name was Mighty-Elk
in other words, a hospital
part of a prelude
for burial-chord; some of these

remains lies behind
at the store
Yesterday we met a young Benjamin
over soapy Turkish coffee
preaching on death
in Athens, of bridges
of choral, his attribution as
well, and probable
re-rooting of sense
(so-called)

Sometimes we are at war
"whose feet were cold
as any stone." A fright
and hollow effect
with their lobes turned outward.
Yesterday I met a young Benjamin,

a physician, and a horn;
the horn filled the room
warning the nowadays to hump
about the effects
of war. All his parched
lobes perhaps
as well, etc., all
that was finally heard
and most

I dreamed about the city
3-D-clay-model
ing, in rows, step
the devil, the Disney
arches of Munich, moral
lapses in the wreck, another face.
The stains or lack
of of war

Amorgos Bay, tacit, popular
the list of dismembered
parts much-used
dogs, rosy-cross
hatched hinge, leather
no-man's land, wallet
of 12th cen., alive
liturgical, Baron, far less
variety and nowadays
and how

There are three kinds of Bridges:

Red, colloquial, sterile
dogs and Greeks, an
authentic finitude; Mikis Theodorakis
travel by hovercraft

from Piraeus to Oakland
thence by Sandbar
in a manner deforming
as well off diminutive
portage to support
suspend bridges
of the manner, the graffiti
and reserves territory
or of ideas sacrilized
and threatened

so the stone was
silent too, it was
quiet on the left
—came, came big
on the right
along like nowhere
the right is pink
blooming wild/
no eyes, the cousins
God help us
they've got eyes
and a station for
the borrowed one
went into the strobe lights
the veil will recall
an outdoor terrace

...

not lost, yet

in spite of this

in their eyes

and mouth

with glaciers

the Green-and-White the

I hear this

accident

the veil I

that was burning

on the stone where I

cousin, here we're

frozen I with

the Turk's-cap on left

you there, we with

our sticks, our names

intervene, but it's

the same the creature

has on on the left

those not loved

—who said "surging, glittering"

"coat and trousers"

"called hazards of bodies"

the gaze true or false
well, no flood of blood
be (prey) dead gift
when having a birthday

filled with fishing boats

"called hazards of bodies"

or to thumb jouissance
starts bleeding
yet a closed grotesque
Greek, judge and brutes

memory on dance
Piraeus has that too

"called hazards of bodies"

at each end ark
dinner for me/ easily
and discretion of a boat, let's say
every time I saw red

I wrote you a letter

and Theo Yorgos has talked about reading

revolver/ that's right
your hat/ it's O.K
my little percentage/ cut it
your role/ soft-hearted pimp
the means/ atomizer
pivoting/ if I had a veil

…all I've got to protect me is the marble…

Portions of this poem are quoted or reworked from texts by Stacy Doris, Jean Genet, Michael Palmer, Benjamin Hollander, and Bhanu Kapil.

ͻ ͻ ͻ ͻ

Excerpts from *The Islands* have appeared in *New American Writing*, *Bombay Gin*, *MiPOesias*, *Transfer*, *Blowfish*, *Little Red Leaves*, *Meloncholia's Tremulous Dreadlocks*, *Try*, *Spell*, *Small Town*, *Zafusy*, *Mirage #4 Period(ical)*, *Kulture Vulture* and *Shampoo*.

A selection from *The Islands* "The Moveable Ones" was published as a chapbook from Transmission Press.

A Naropa Collaboration between the MFA in Contemporary Performance and the MFA in Writing And Poetics (2006) adapted and staged a poem from *The Islands* "said the moth" for their annual Embodied Poetics performance. "said the moth" was directed by Wendell Beavers and Ethelyn Friend.

Nightboat Books, a nonprofit organization, seeks to develop audiences for writers whose work resists convention and transcends boundaries. We publish books rich with poignancy, intelligence, and risk. Please visit our website, www.nightboat.org, to learn about our titles and
how you can support our future publications.

This book was made possible by grants from The Fund for Poetry and the Topanga Fund, which is dedicated to promoting the arts and literature of California.

The following individuals have supported the publication of this book. We thank them for their generosity and commitment to the mission of Nightboat Books:

Kazim Ali
Elizabeth Motika
Benjamin Taylor

In addition, this book has been made possible, in part, by a grant from the New York State Council on the Arts Literature Program.

NYSCA